Letters To Heaven

A Word Written by Genesis Espinal

I write these
Letters To
Heaven,
In hopes that
They listen.

Table of Contents

In the Beginning
was the Word,

And the Word was
with God,
And the Word was
God…
And the Word was
Good,
The Word was
Light,
A Light that shines
Forever,
A Light fulfilling
Life.

This is the sequel to a very different story. In essence, they're the same story. They're my story.

This is the sequel I didn't think I'd live to tell. This sequel is testament to how I've thrived after all I have survived.

I wrote to Heaven.

I wrote, I sobbed, I prayed, I healed. Every word on these pages healed the pieces broken in my prequel.

This is my Gospel.

Allow me to share the Good News:

We are Loved to the Highest Power.

Favor Within Me

My hands, they paint,
The picture you give me,
The vision you have.
My eyes, they deceive
me.

My vision is limited,
Your word: the guide;
Sometimes a whisper too
low.

I don't see, I don't hear.
I don't fear.

I'm in the palm of your

hand,

My arms open,

Accepting,

Everything you

promised,

The culmination of your

plan.

The Dagger

In the place I survived,

Now seeing how I've

thrived.

Here I laid,

Like Juliet after Romeo.

Here I survived,

Unlike Juliet,

I'm alive.

Grace

I look at my scars,

And wonder how I

survived.

What could I have done,

To deserve grace?

I cut through life,

Bleeding out hope,

A caged bird without

wings,

A doll hanging on to

strings.

I fell to my knees and

wept,

Begging for it to end.

So today I wonder,

Why?

How?

What did I do,

To deserve this grace?

13

Completely Incomplete

I don't know what I see

But I know it's meant to
be

That life I dream

The life I'm seeing

The I don't know how

I don't know when

Nor do I know why

But it will be

I see what will be

So I don't know what I
see

But it's coming to me.

To See Is To Die

A little magnifying glass,
On the tiniest page,
Filled with the smallest
words.

Sentences so minute,
They're confused with
lines.

The magnifying glass,
Within the magnifying
glass,
The only way to read
through.

Then the words light up,
The page now ablaze.

The little multi lens
glare,
Used light too bright,
That burned.

Tell Me When

I'm drowning in what's
missing,
Hoping for what's to be.
Drowning in a volcano of
gold,
Burning through all I've
got.
Tell me, when is the
time?
When is this going to
stop?
When is the change
going to start?

When will it all solidify,

So bit by bit I can chip
away,

All the blockage in my
way?

When will it stop?

When will it start?

The Water Cycle

You don't have to try to
be;
Only breathe,
Because you already are.
You believe what you
want,
So believe the illusion,
Dive into your delusion.
Believe the sun is
always, always…
Behind the clouds.
The sun is always above
the clouds.
The sun is always,
There.

Dark and heavy storms,

Sun.

Light and airy days,

Sun.

Dark and heavy storms,

Light and airy days;

Sun,

The common

denominator.

The cycle.

Just be.

Just breathe.

Little Slice

One day you'll come
across,
A perfectly hidden hole
in the wall,
An oasis with gems
you've never seen,
A life you've never
dreamed.
One day you'll stumble
in,
Your whole perfect
picture,
Your beloved little
secret,
Your little slice of
heaven.

Delivery Failed

I wrote you a letter,

I wrote you a word;

A compilation of my

sorrows,

Dressed in Sunday's

best,

A coded message,

For your eyes to

decipher.

But on Sundays the

postmaster,

Saves his strength and

rests;

The words are left

undelivered,

A story left unsaid.

No

How can I be:

The cause,

The solution,

The demise,

The revival?

How can I break:

Into the mold,

Into the space,

Into the line,

Into the fold?

How can I squeeze:

Past the stars,

Past the horizon,

Past the moon,

Past the sun?

How do I know so much,
But know nothing,
Absolutely nothing,
At all?

Please?

I'll look for you
wherever you go,
Find you in places
unseen,
Feel you across the sky,
Let you guide me to the
other side.

I'll listen for you
wherever you are,
Open my thoughts to
your heart,
Face and follow your
words,
Let you guide me to the
other side.

I'll speak to you

wherever you stay,

Talk, whisper, yell,

Entirely with my soul,

A sound won't escape

my lips.

Can I guide you to my

side?

You Were

Years before my first
breath,
God sent you on a
journey,
Your own walk on earth.
He knew that you'd find
me,
He knew that I'd need
you,
Placed you right in my
life,
So my first breath would
meet your last,
The culmination of a
heavenly plan.

Nice to Meet You

No one existed before
you.
They're all fragments,
Pieces of you.
You were there,
Before you were.
In my thoughts,
Before I knew.
In my soul,
As I know.
Before you nothing.
With you,
Everything.

The Compass Broke

Spinning, spinning,

spinning,

To the true north.

Spinning, spinning,

To the truth.

Spinning,

Somewhere.

Lost.

Somewhere,

Spinning,

To the truth.

Spinning, spinning,

To the true north.

Spinning, spinning,

spinning.

Your Harp

An instrument of the
sweetest sound,
A soul touching melody,
So profound.

Playing the smoothest
notes,
An intricate piece;
Creating,
Radiating,
Heartfelt peace.

An instrument of the
sweetest sound,
Holding you,
Caressing you,

Leading you,

Exalting you,

To a throne just for you,

Sitting in the clouds.

Behind the Shadows

I'm not afraid,

For I know he walks for

me,

Cries for me,

Yearns for me,

Loves for me,

Unconditionally.

I have no fear because,

I'm perfect in his eyes,

Lovely in his heart,

Eternally his favorite

part.

I am

Everything

He is.

He is,

Everything,

For me.

33

Ego Death

Release me from my

super ego,

The center of my

universe.

Release me from my self,

The last one standing.

Release me from my ego,

The middle of the dance.

Relieve me of who I am,

Take my self away from

me.

Dance with my morals,

Dream with my

conscience;

My super ego colliding.

My ego crashing;

My self,

Being less.

Just How Good

You'll never know just

how

Beautiful it was.

How raw, organic,

Everything felt.

How sweet and fresh

Everything tasted.

You'll never know just

how

Pure it was.

Now everything is toxic.

We're dying.

Being poisoned.

We'll never know just

how

Good it was.

IN THE MIDDLE

In the middle,

In a limbo,

A dance between two

lines,

A back and forth,

A throw and catch,

A conjunction of two

sides.

Neither here nor there,

Yet somehow

everywhere,

And nowhere all the
same.

No Title Yet

The apple of my eye,

An embodiment of

temptation,

The sweetest smile,

With the deadliest trap;

Just what the doctor

ordered,

A treasure for my

troubles.

Act one, the exposition;

The sweetest smile,

An embodiment of

temptation,

The apple of my eye.

Steps

How can you get to the
moon,
Without bringing the
stars?
How can the sun shine
for you,
Without a source of
power?
How can a flower bloom
for you,
Without sufficient water?
How can a harvest be
ready for you,
If you don't sow where
you reaped?

How can you get more,

The sum of everything,

All together at once,

With a little more than

nothing?

A Piece of Understanding

How can I be at peace,

If I don't know?

It doesn't make sense.

How can I find peace,

In a literal mess?

A world of unknowns.

How can I know peace,

When it doesn't add up?

Unsolvable math.

How can I know what I

can't,

But understand that I

don't

But still,

I don't know,

I don't know peace.

43

Witness

You were witness,

To the love spoken in

five languages.

You were witness,

To the fatherly bond God

created.

You are witness,

To everything I am.

You are witness,

To the way it all ties in,

To the steps never

missed,

To the whispered

fantasies, alive.

You are witness,

To the love spoken in

five languages,

To the love that

surrounds me.

You are witness.

45

Last Time Home

I wish I could forget,

A day engrained in my
head,

A pain stuck in my heart,

A yearning stemming

from my soul.

I wish I could forget,

Your last cry,

The way my body shot

up,

Tensed up;

The way my mind

jumped into action.

I wish I could relive,

The time before you left.

I see a single line of

footsteps ahead,

Knowing every day is

another day,

Further from when I had

you.

My God, My God

Thou has not forsaken

me.

You breathe life into my

dreams;

Dreams into my life.

You gave me these

hands,

To use and create;

To build a treehouse,

Piece by piece,

So the thing with

feathers,

Can perch on my soul,

While it sings the words
you speak,
The music full of silent
notes,
A song of never-ending
love,
That never stops at all.

49

Perfect Standstill

The divinity of it all,

So real it's surreal.

Yes, it exists,

Tightly in my fist.

It's a reverie;

A vision,

A minute in the

multiverse,

A reflection,

Of what I see.

A mirror room,

With me at the center.

A Bed of Daffodils

Where Narcissus fell
A flower grew
A new beginning
Life born anew.

From the ashes of his
bones,
He grew leaves,
Into a flower he
sprouted,
Roots grounded.

The hissing echo of a
snake,

Wrapped around his

stem,

Heard from miles away,

Gave the flower a welt.

Through the reflection of

the lake,

The place where

Narcissus lay,

Bloomed a garden,

All of the same flower,

A silent echo of protest.

Where Narcissus fell

Many flowers grew,

Many new beginnings,

Life born anew.

Mi Padre en el Cielo

Me pasaba mañanas
contigo,
Noches contigo,
Tardes contigo.
Te hablaba de todo;
De mi dolor,
De mis sueños,
De mis ideas,
De mis poemas.
Compartí todo contigo;
El cambio que quería
ver,
Del cambio que quería
hacer.
Compartí tazas de café,

El humo del cigarrillo;

Un amor que se vive,

Una sola vez.

Nadie puede entender,

Las formas en que,

Me hiciste bien.

Como cargaste mi

corazón,

En tus lindas manos.

Me llenaste un vació,

De un dolor que no

merecía.

My Father in Heaven

I spent mornings with
you,
Nights with you,
Afternoons with you.
I talked to you about
everything;
Of my pain,
Of my dreams,
Of my ideas,
Of my poems.
I shared everything with
you;
The change I wanted to
see,

Of the change I wanted

to make.

I shared cups of coffee,

The cigarette smoke;

A love that is lived,

Only once.

No one can understand,

The ways in which,

You did me good.

As you carried my heart,

In your beautiful hands.

You filled my void,

A pain that I didn't

deserve.

May Flowers

Sunshine after rain,

The soft sound of birds,

Whispering the secrets

Of their view.

Sunshine in the rain,

The soft droplets of

water,

Touching the light

Just right.

Sunshine before the rain,

The soft caress of the

breeze,

Carrying the secrets,

The heavens share.

Secrets flying,

Droplets of water,

Birds Eye magnified.

Just like that,

You are to me,

You're an endless

walking epiphany.

A canary that landed,

Whispering all its

secrets,

Straight into my ear.

A canary that flew,

Followed a journey,

En el mes de abril,

Watering the flowers,

That will bloom in May.

Mi Héroe

My hero,

My angel;

Ethereal energy,

Walking along my path.

The ruby shoes I wear to

you,

Light up with joy.

I don't have to guess,

You're my guide.

The light,

My hero,

My angel.

Art to the Third Power

How can I deny

The existence of a

Creative?

When I see art,

Around me,

Within me,

Radiating from me?

How can I deny,

The existence of a master

artist,

The one eye for detail;

The master of gentle

brushstrokes,

Of the painting I live in?

How can I deny,

The existence of a

conductor,

Composer of the dolce

symphony;

The energy buzzing

around?

How can I deny,

The existence of a

Creative,

When art is alive?

I Didn't Lie

I couldn't bring myself to
do it,
All I saw was pain.
Yours,
Hers,
Theirs.
I couldn't bring myself to
do it,
I couldn't be a part of a
tragic play.
I hope now you can see,
My I love you's were
never in vain.
But I couldn't bring
myself to do it.

I couldn't face the truth,

Until the truth was in my

face,

I couldn't look away.

It was right in my face.

Lifeless,

Peaceful,

Painful.

I couldn't bring myself to

do it,

Now I'm stuck in

purgatory,

Cleansing myself of sins.

Writing In Color

She wrote until the words
bled through the paper.
She wrote,
And wrote,
And wrote,
Until life changed.
Then, she painted.
Words were no longer
enough,
To describe the feelings
she felt.
Words were no longer
enough,
To whisper the sorrows
of her heart.

She painted,
And painted.
And painted.

She painted until the
colors bled through the
canvas,
Until the colors brought
her life;
Resurrected from a mess.
She wrote,
And she painted;
Looking for salvation,
Hoping.

Fall From Grace

It was like watching my
world crumble,
The stars fall down,
The air disappearing,
The ground sinking,
Water burning;
All in slow motion.

My hero never lost faith,
But you were different.
You resigned.
Your mind floated away,
Gravity too weak to hold
you down…
Despacio,
Todo rapido.

It was like watching my

world crumble,

The stars fall down,

The air disappearing,

The ground sinking,

Water burning;

Me, losing.

67

Quiet Escape

I hear you,

As if you never left,

Calling my name,

Telling me things,

That you know I'll be

great one day.

I hear you,

But you left me.

Your echoes follow me,

Travel with me,

Across every finish line.

I hear you,

But you're not here.

Somehow your words
stuck with me,
Somehow your faith
clings onto me;
But your love I can't
feel,
Because you left me.

I'm stranded,
Calling your name,
Shouting your name,
Whispering your name.

Can you come back,
And hold my hand?

BeginningtoEnd

Rooted in myself

Using my shifts to grow,

To create.

Keeping it all together,

Intact one body,

Carrying celestial beings

in my soul.

I rise, I set.

I go through phases and

disappear.

I grow and never fret;

Everything there is to

offer,

Is here.

Cups of Water

I will ride this wave.

I will not allow it to wash

me to shore.

I can't control the waters,

But I can control myself.

Inside me there is power,

To overcome the rain,

That crashes on the

surface,

And joins in with the

waves.

I am stronger than the

current,

The forceful movement

beneath me,

Stronger than the winds

above me.

I will ride this wave,

All the way to victory.

Yo soy victoriosa en

todas mis aguas.

Is That You?

I see a dream unravel,

A painting come to life;

A vision so far,

It's mute.

Everything leads to that

moment.

I'm beginning to

understand,

Gold can only bend,

In so many ways.

What is to be,

Is too heavy for this load,

So to have that,

This I have to let go.

No burden is too heavy
to carry,
But the goal is far
fetched.
So I can reach it faster,
I try to cheat in ways,
But that makes it harder;
So I can't.
I literally can't.

No burden is too heavy
to carry me,
Exactly where I'm
headed;
What I carry is what'll
lead me,
To the finish line that's
drawn.

So no more burden will
be added,
One way or another.
If I want to get there,
I need to get through
here.

The heavier it gets,
The further away I am;
But the closer I feel,
The lighter it is.

A burden of the perfect
weight;
Light for the distance to
be traveled.

It doesn't drag me down,
Doesn't slow me down.
I know there's no easier
way.

The dream will unravel,
And all I will ask,
"God, is that you?"

Reclaimed

A brisk routine walk,
Paired with random
excitement,
A quiet wish come true.

Sprung and alive now,
Sprouting through the
rough concrete,
Watered by sweetness.

A soft time for growth,
A brief heartwarming
moment,
Everlasting hope.

Open Field

I'm looking for that open
path,
The field without the
thorns,
Golgotha without the
skulls,
With a destination of
freedom.
I'm looking for that open
path,
The road where the rays
of the sun,
Touch the light inside;
Where the heavens open,
Leading me to a throne,
Resting in the room,

That was made for me;

Just for me.

Raison D'être

Making sense of the

mess I fall in,

Rationalizing every sin,

Logic draping noise with

hymn,

Beauty dripping from

within,

The cup runneth over my

tall fountain.

Daylight Savings

I spring forward,

To a reality un-warped.

I spring toward,

A time that makes sense,

Lines unbent.

I spring forward,

To a place where I,

Can see with the eye,

In the middle of my

mind,

What things are

And what they're not.

I spring toward,

A meadow of clouds,

A quiet little house,

Flowers all around;

Blooming,

Growing,

In its natural order.

Things are how they are.

See You There

Will we be reunited in

the

Garden of Eden?

Will our hands touch in

spirit,

Souls of a body?

Will your rib return to

my right,

And our breath become

one?

When we meet at the

Garden of Eden, will you

remember me?

Our story will circle
complete,
Our innocence born
anew.
Find me at the Garden of
Eden,
Where our story began.
Where it will be,
continuously,
perpetually,
eternally:
A revelation.

Clay

I breathed life into you,

I saw that you were

good,

For God sent you to me.

With you,

He sent a new beginning.

He took the rib from my

left,

And molded it to you,

For you,

Just right.

To know you is to know

love,

To know love is to love

me.

A part of me apart from
me,
Apart from me is a part
of me.
The bright light you
bring,
Reflecting on everything.

You showed up when I
needed,
Overshadowed,
Illuminated,
By the white skies.

86

Really? Really.

The mist of the clouds,

Shaping the sounds,

The coquis singing,

With the earth listening;

An image drenched in

secrets.

It's so hard to believe it!

How does this even

exist?

How has art come alive?

An image drenched in

secrets;

Too good to believe it.

Denial

I'm riding down the Nile,

Looking for sharks,

Where alligators roam.

I know it's in my mind…

The block in the road is:

How my mind unwinds.

The direction of the

river,

A path of abstract art,

Is the twisted way it

blinds.

Unsure if what I feel is

true…

Can I trust a compass
once broken?;
A tempest of its own
kind.
Can I trust that on my
River,
Mirages are far away?
Can I trust,
The map,
I drew?

Petals

Flowers from a friend,
Meets roses from my
lover,
Petals full of hope.

A garden of love,
Copulates with the sun,
Creating much more.

The heavens open,
Singing angels walk to
me,
Paradise is here.

Artiste

Je suis une artiste;

And this is my

masterpiece.

The way the River of

Emotions,

Guides my hand,

Putting on paper,

The images beyond my

eyes,

Which my soul yearns

for eternally,

I can't see but I can feel.

I know;

And I don't.

But I am.

I definitely am.

91

Salt in my Eyes

As I'm floating with the
waves,
A splash of water falls on
my face.
The sun is in my eyes,
Meshed with the salt of
the sea.
I lose my balance for a
second,
Casually flipping over.
I swim,
I tread,
I breathe,
I float again.
Lost then found,
Panic into peace.

I'm one with myself,

As I'm floating with the

waves.

Sunset to Night

High in the sky

Slowly falling

Turning

Changing

Painting.

Low in the sky

Preparing

Paving

Undressing

Cloaking.

Low in the sky

Hiding

Poised

Ready.

High in the sky

Illuminating

Glowing

Full.

All around the sky

Sparkling brightly

Selective appearance

A jubilee of celestials.

Light into dark,

The dance of Heavens.

Daydreams

I stand so brightly in the
sun,
As its object of
adoration.
I'm daydreaming of the
sun,
kissing my cheeks,
with the sound of the sea,
and the soft crashing of
the waves;
a light warm breeze,
and the scent of peace,
you only sense at the
beach.

I'm the sun's favorite

detail,

Helio's masterpiece,

I'm geocentric to his

orbit.

It Was Good

God said let there be

Light,

And you walked in;

Apollo,

Vulcan,

Ares,

Lucifer

As one.

Rest

Oh am I glad,

It didn't end that day.

I am glad I awoke to see,

Another sunrise,

The start of a day.

I smile every time I leave

home,

Knowing I have a place I

can leave.

I cry every time I come

home,

Knowing I have a place

to return.

I sit in my dimly lit safe

space,

My breath of fresh air,

My hug without hands.
I'm enveloped in
warmth,
Surrounded by love.
A place I know true to be
mine,
A place I belong,
A place I call home.
A place where my peace
Comes easily to me.
I no longer have to chase
silence.
A place tranquil waters,
Rock me to sleep.
A place I know,
I'm safe.

Every
Ending is
a new
Beginning.